EVERYTHING SPACE

NATIONAL GEOGRAPHIC
WASHINGTON, D.C.

NATIONAL GEOGRAPHIC KiDS

EVERYTHING SPACE

HELAINE BECKER

With National Geographic Explorer BRENDAN MULLAN

CONTENTS

Clouds of water-vapor exhaust surround the launch of a National Aeronautics and Space Administration (NASA) space shuttle at Kennedy Space Center in Florida, U.S.A.

Our galaxy, the spiral-shaped Milky Way, has more than 200 billion stars and is about 13.6 billion years old.

INTRODUCTION

OUTER SPACE IS BOTH
INFINITELY VAST AND INFINITELY SMALL.

It includes galaxies many light-years across, and tinier-than-tiny photons—the particles that make up sunlight and other forms of energy. Space is the universe and our sun and its planets, as well as galaxies, comets, black holes, white dwarves, and millions of other things beyond the bounds of our home planet, Earth.

An endless source of wonder with mind-boggling limits, space has fascinated humans for many thousands of years. Who doesn't want to know what's out there in the night sky? Space exploration began with simple observations of the stars, and it progressed to humans walking on the moon and probes searching beyond our solar system. Space adventurers dream of peering over the rim of a black hole or hitching a ride on a spaceship to the farthest reaches of our galaxy.

So strap on your seat belt, prepare to watch stars being born, and learn how to listen for life in distant galaxies. Take a wild ride and discover some of the infinite mysteries of space.

EXPLORER'S CORNER

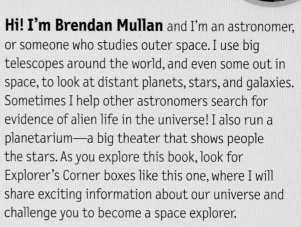

Hi! I'm Brendan Mullan and I'm an astronomer, or someone who studies outer space. I use big telescopes around the world, and even some out in space, to look at distant planets, stars, and galaxies. Sometimes I help other astronomers search for evidence of alien life in the universe! I also run a planetarium—a big theater that shows people the stars. As you explore this book, look for Explorer's Corner boxes like this one, where I will share exciting information about our universe and challenge you to become a space explorer.

Earth is a planet orbiting the sun, which is part of the Milky Way galaxy. The Milky Way is part of the Local Group of galaxies that is part of the Virgo supercluster—an even larger group of galaxies.

OUR SPACE NEIGHBORHOOD

WHAT IS SPACE?

WHAT IN THE WORLD IS SPACE?
THAT'S A FAMOUSLY HARD QUESTION TO ANSWER.

The simple answer is that space is everything in the universe beginning about 62 miles (100 km) above Earth. Of course, to astronomers and astrophysicists, the scientists who study space, it is much more. It's a never-ending mystery.

WHAT IS A PLANET?

A planet is a large body of rock, gas, and other material orbiting a star in space. Some planets are small and rocky, such as Mercury. Others are huge and gassy, such as Jupiter. A planet can have one or more moons that orbit around it.

TROPOSPHERE

STRATOSPHERE

MESOSPHERE

THERMOSPHERE

EXOSPHERE

WHAT IS THE ATMOSPHERE?

Some planets, such as Earth, have an atmosphere, or a layer of gases that surrounds and protects them. Earth's atmosphere has five main layers. The outermost layer, called the exosphere, merges with outer space.

How vast is our atmosphere? The portion closest to Earth, called the troposphere, extends 5 to 7 miles (8 to 11 km) at the poles and 10 miles (16 km) at the equator. Airplanes and jets fly in the troposphere. By contrast, some satellites are launched into the exosphere, the uppermost region of Earth's atmosphere, which begins about 300 miles (500 km) above Earth.

GALACTIC FACT OUR SOLAR SYSTEM IS 4.6 BILLION YEARS OLD.

WHAT IS A GALAXY?

A galaxy is a collection of stars and planets held together by gravity. Galaxies can take different shapes. For example, the Milky Way galaxy, the galaxy we Earthlings live in, is a spiral galaxy. That means it is shaped like a whirlpool in which stars, planets, and all other materials rotate around a central point. Some galaxies are shaped like a watermelon, or like a tadpole with a round head and a trailing tail. There are also double and multiple galaxies, where more than one galaxy is linked together.

WHAT ISN'T A PLANET?

Until fairly recently, there was no clear definition of the term "planet." Scientists agreed that our solar system had nine of them. But then they discovered plenty of additional objects orbiting the sun. Were these objects planets too? New rules and definitions were needed.

In 2006 the International Astronomical Union, a group of scientists who list space-related discoveries, defined a planet as follows:

- It must orbit a star.
- It must be round.
- It must have cleared the surrounding area of other large objects through its gravitational pull.
- It must not be a moon—a solid object that orbits a planet.

This definition meant Pluto, our solar system's ninth planet, no longer qualified as a planet. Pluto had not cleared its neighborhood of other objects.

UNIVERSALLY SPEAKING ...

If the universe was a cup, everything would be inside it, even the cup itself! That's because the universe is everything. You, me, the sun, and all the stars in the sky are part of it. If you think that's a head-scratcher, consider this strange fact: The universe keeps getting bigger!

IT'S ALL GREEK TO ME

The ancient Greeks spent a lot of time studying stars, space, and the solar system. They also named planets and some stars. The word "planet" comes from the Greek word *planete*, meaning "wanderer." The prefix "astro-" is Greek and refers to anything having to do with stars and space. Astronauts are explorers who "sail among the stars."

OUR NEIGHBORHOOD

THINK OF A SOLAR SYSTEM

AS A NEIGHBORHOOD, OR A DISTINCT PART OF town. Every neighborhood has its own characteristics, but each one also shares features with other neighborhoods. For example, all solar systems have a central star. Our central star is the sun, which is sometimes called "Sol."

MEET THE NEIGHBORS

Eight planets orbit, or circle, the sun at different distances and speeds. The first group of planets, the inner group, includes the four planets closest to the sun. In order, they are Mercury, Venus, Earth, and Mars. A belt of asteroids separates these four inner planets from the four outer planets: Jupiter, Saturn, Uranus, and Neptune.

FOLLOW THE SUN

Sol, our central star, is at the center of our solar system. The sun is a massively hot, massively dense ball of gases. It is by far the largest and hottest object in our solar system. It provides light and heat energy, and various forms of radiation, to all of the planets.

MERCURY

Mercury is the smallest planet and closest to the sun. You might think it's unbelievably hot all the time, but Mercury has a thin atmosphere that does not help redistribute the sun's heat. This causes wild temperature fluctuations. The side of Mercury that faces the sun is around 806°F (430°C), while the side facing away is minus 261°F (-163°C).

VENUS

As the second rock from the sun, Venus is Earth's closest neighbor planet. It is similar to Earth in size and mass. But because of its thick atmosphere, it is also the hottest planet in our solar system. Temperatures on Venus's rocky surface never go below 863°F (462°C).

EARTH: OUR HOME PLANET

At 93 million miles (150 million km) away, Earth is exactly the right distance from the sun. Here, the temperature is just right to allow water to remain in its liquid form. Any closer, and it would evaporate. Any farther away, and it would freeze solid. In fact, 71 percent of Earth's surface is covered by water.

SUN

VENUS

MERCURY

EARTH

MARS

ASTEROID BELT

JUPITER

GALACTIC FACT MOST OF THE PLANETS ARE NAMED AFTER CHARACTERS FROM GREEK OR ROMAN MYTHOLOGY.

MARS

Mars is known as the "red planet." It is one of four terrestrial, or rocky, planets in the solar system. The red appearance of Mars is caused by iron oxide, or rust, in the soil.

JUPITER

The fifth planet from the sun, Jupiter, is a gas giant. This means it is made up of gases and liquids that most likely surround a core of hot, thick "soup" instead of solid rock. Its atmosphere is composed of turbulent clouds of chemical gases that swirl in massive storms. Jupiter has 50 known moons, but scientists believe there are at least 17 more.

SATURN

A massive ball of gases, Saturn does not have a solid surface. The planet is best known for its rings. The nine continuous rings, plus other arcs, are made of rock, ice, and dust. Saturn also has at least 62 moons. One of its moons, Titan, is larger than the planet Mercury.

URANUS

The seventh planet from the sun, and the third largest in diameter, Uranus was only discovered in 1781. That's thousands of years after many of the other planets.

NEPTUNE

The farthest planet from the sun, Neptune, like its neighbor Uranus, is called an "ice giant." It is made up of gases, ice, and rock. Temperatures on the planet are beyond frosty.

SATURN

URANUS

NEPTUNE

NOW THAT'S A BIG BELT!

The two groups of planets are divided by an asteroid belt. It's a 200-million-mile- (320-million-km)-wide ring of massive rocks that are too small to be planets. Beyond the outer planets is a region called the Kuiper belt. It contains small, icy dwarf planets, such as Pluto, and other smaller bodies. A dwarf planet is an orbiting object that is about the same size as a planet but has not cleared its orbit of other orbiting objects.

MEET OUR MOON

Earth's moon, sometimes called "Luna," is a barren, lifeless rock about one quarter the size of Earth. It was formed four billion years ago when protoplanet Thea crashed into Earth. The collision caused a cataclysmic explosion where rock spewed far into space. When the rock cooled, it joined into a tidy sphere. Caught by Earth's gravity, the sphere became Earth's satellite.

By the Numbers

164.8 years is the time it takes for Neptune to make one complete orbit of the sun.

365 days is the time it takes for Earth to make one complete orbit of the sun.

4.5 billion years ago Earth was created from a mass of dust and rock.

14 billion years ago the universe came into existence.

200 million years is the time is takes for the Milky Way to rotate once around its center.

STUDY THE STARS

IMAGINE LOOKING INTO

AN INSTRUMENT AND SEEING GALAXIES

hundreds of light-years away. From observatories around the world, astronomers scan the sky 24/7 using a wide array of large telescopes. Telescopes magnify distant objects by gathering their light. Some record radio waves, and others, energy fluctuations. Most observatories are located high in the mountains away from the light pollution of cities. Earth's observatories open a window to the heavens through which we can catch a glimpse of the universe.

EXPLORER'S CORNER

Being an astronomer is an adventure! You can travel across the world to distant observatories in exotic locations. You can hike mountains, meet new friends, try new foods, and stay up all night! But if you'd rather stay put, you can actually control many of the telescopes in these observatories over the Internet, from the comfort of your own home. Imagine taking and making world-changing observations about the universe at home—in your pajamas!

Alaska (U.S.)

NORTH AMERICA

UNITED STATES

Hawai'i (U.S.)

ARECIBO OBSERVATORY

The Arecibo Observatory in Puerto Rico, U.S.A., is home to one of the most sensitive radio telescopes on Earth. It can zero in on any radio signal within just a few minutes. The Arecibo telescope has been featured in Hollywood movies, and it has also been used in the search for extraterrestrial life.

W. M. KECK OBSERVATORY

The W. M. Keck Observatory on Mauna Kea, Hawai'i, U.S.A., was the first to give computers control of the telescopes. The computers could perform multiple adjustments per second. That gave astronomers precise control over their field of vision. Today, the Mauna Kea observatory complex is the largest array of optical, infrared, and submillimeter astronomical equipment in the world.

Puerto Rico (U.S.)

SOUTH AMERICA

ALMA

The ALMA telescope, which stands for Atacama Large Millimeter/submillimeter Array, is a group of telescopes located in the high and dry Atacama Desert of Chile. Its high altitude—16,404 feet (5,000 m) above sea level—makes it ideal for astronomy, because the atmosphere that high up is extremely thin. That allows for better telescope observation of space objects. The clear desert skies also make it one of the best places on Earth for stargazing.

CHILE

ARECIBO OBSERVATORY

ROYAL OBSERVATORY

The Royal Observatory, in Greenwich, England, was founded by King Charles II in 1675 and functioned as a working observatory until the 1950s. It's situated on the prime meridian, a line of longitude that is the official starting point for measuring distance east and west around the Earth. Today, the observatory is a museum, with a planetarium for watching light shows about the stars.

GRAN TELESCOPIO CANARIAS

UNITED KINGDOM — England

EUROPE

SPAIN

Canary Islands (SPAIN)

AFRICA

ASIA

INDIA

INDIAN ASTRONOMICAL OBSERVATORY

Located at an altitude of 14,764 feet (4,500 m) on a mountain in the western Himalaya, the Indian Astronomical Observatory is one of the world's highest observatories. It is also the most advanced center for astronomy in Asia.

SALT

The South African Large Telescope (SALT) is the largest ground-based telescope in the Southern Hemisphere. It takes "snapshots" of stars in quick succession so astronomers can study rapidly changing compact stars. This helps them to detect black holes. SALT has also made observations of a particular type of supernova that showed that the expansion of the universe is speeding up.

EQUATOR

| 0 | 2,000 miles |

| 0 | 2,000 kilometers |

SOUTH AFRICA

AUSTRALIA

GRAN TELESCOPIO CANARIAS

This telescope, located on the Canary Islands of Spain, is one of the largest ground-based telescopes. It can capture images of distant galaxies, planets that orbit other stars like our sun, and black holes. The observatory has a CanariCam—a camera that can filter out bright starlight to make fainter space objects easier to see.

ALMA TELESCOPE

ICECUBE NEUTRINO OBSERVATORY

The IceCube Neutrino Observatory is fittingly located in Antarctica. Its mission is to study neutrinos, mysterious subatomic particles that come from the sun or are the result of violent events in the galaxy. The telescope examines neutrinos for clues to space mysteries, such as black holes and exploding stars. The IceCube telescope is unusual because it is buried in sea ice about 8,038 feet (2,450 m) below the polar ice surface. At that depth, there are no bubbles in the ice. It's also very dark. These factors make it easier to record neutrino activity without interference.

ANTARCTICA

GALACTIC FACT   LAUNCHED IN 1990, NASA'S HUBBLE TELESCOPE IS ONE OF THE LARGEST SPACE TELESCOPES.

FAR-OUT SPACE

SPACE IS REALLY, REALLY,
REALLY BIG. HOW BIG? THINK ABOUT IT THIS

way: Our sun is just one of 400 billion stars in the Milky Way galaxy. The Milky Way belongs to a group of neighboring galaxies called the Local Group. Each galaxy in the Local Group contains hundreds of billions of stars. The Local Group is part of the Virgo supercluster. It, in turn, is part of another, larger supercluster called Laniakea. These clusters are only a small portion of the observable universe. Phew! And that's just one measure of the enormity of space.

EVER EXPANDING

EDWIN HUBBLE

During the 1920s, scientist Edwin Hubble discovered that other galaxies weren't staying still. They were racing away from us! This observation led to a dramatic discovery: The universe is constantly expanding. And the expansion is happening faster and faster. The reason why it is speeding up remains a mystery.

IN WITH A BANG

Scientists believe an event called the "big bang" marked the beginning of our universe. Astronomers think the big bang occurred 13.8 billion years ago. At that time, the entire universe was contained in a bubble smaller than the period at the end of this sentence. It suddenly exploded and has continued to expand ever since.

GALACTIC FACT   BESIDES THE SUN, ALPHA CENTAURI IS THE CLOSEST STAR TO US. IT IS 4.38 LIGHT-YEARS FROM EARTH.

ANDROMEDA

GALAXY NEXT DOOR

The Milky Way is the second largest galaxy in the Local Group. Andromeda, our closest galactic neighbor, is the largest. It's moving fast and—*gulp!*—on a collision course with the Milky Way! But don't worry. The cosmic crash won't take place for another four billion years.

STRANGE GALAXIES

BIRD GALAXY

Not all galaxies are alike. They don't even look alike when viewed from a space telescope. The Sombrero galaxy, for example, is shaped like a traditional Mexican hat. Mayall's object, formed by the collision of two separate galaxies, is shaped like a mushroom. The Tadpole galaxy looks like—you got it—a tadpole. The Bird galaxy bears a striking resemblance to the fairy Tinker Bell!

AN ILLUSTRATED DIAGRAM

THE MILKY WAY

LOOK UP—WAY UP. SEE THAT
BAND OF STARS IN THE MIDDLE OF THE NIGHT SKY?

That's our galaxy, the Milky Way. The Milky Way is just one of many enormous collections of star systems bound together by gravity. There are hundreds of billions—that's right, billions—of other galaxies out there in the universe. Our galaxy has three basic visible components or parts: the halo, the disk, and the central bulge.

ARM

THE HALO

The stars here are the oldest, with some dating back to the beginning of the galaxy, about 13.8 or 14 billion years ago.

THE DISK

Astronomers cannot see the center of the galaxy because of clouds of dust and gas in the disk. The disk is home to many "young" stars. The Milky Way's disk bunched up into spiral arms that contain clusters of young, hot stars.

ARM

THE CENTRAL BULGE (NUCLEUS)

The central bulge is a crowded place. It is home to the highest concentration of stars in the galaxy. Astronomers are pretty sure there's a supermassive black hole there. The black hole has a mass that is about 4 million times the mass of the sun.

THE ARMS

Four spiral arms contain the bulk of the galaxy's stars. They were formed when the universe was about 8 billion years old. The arms are not continuous. Instead, they consist of active star-forming sections surrounded by less active ones made up of gas and dust.

ARM

ARM

NUCLEUS

BLACK HOLES

Stars are massive gas balls that exert an intense gravitational pull. Some collapse in on themselves in great explosions called supernovas when they die. In their place, the stars leave behind a compressed core. The core has so much gravity that it pulls everything nearby into it. The force keeps growing and growing until nothing—not even light itself—can escape. That action creates a hole in space-time called—you guessed it—a black hole.

The edge of the black hole is called the event horizon. Any object that crosses the edge will get pulled into the black hole. Some black holes are powerful enough to consume entire solar systems. Supermassive black holes are so large that entire galaxies rotate around them. A supermassive black hole is at the center of our very own galaxy, the Milky Way.

The Crab Nebula is a remnant of a supernova, or exploding star, that Chinese astronomers first recorded seeing in A.D. 1054. The nebula's center contains a pulsar—a dead star with the mass of the sun but compressed to the size of a city.

2

SECRETS OF THE UNIVERSE

LIGHTS IN THE SKY

WE KNOW THAT
THERE ARE BILLIONS OF

stars in our galaxy and trillions and trillions of stars in the universe. They come in many different sizes and types. Some, like our sun, are small. All stars go through a similar life cycle in which they are born, grow to maturity, then eventually die.

A star's energy makes it appear bright in the night sky.

GREAT BALLS OF FIRE

Most stars are like colossal power plants. They consist mostly of hydrogen and helium, and these two gases act as the star's primary fuel. The star's gravity compresses the gases, making them so dense that they eventually combine in a process called nuclear fusion. That reaction produces incredible amounts of light, heat, and other forms of electromagnetic radiation. At its core, a star's temperature can reach up to 32 million degrees Fahrenheit (18 million degrees Celsius).

SPACE GIANTS AND DWARFS

A red giant is a star that is slowly dying, has exhausted its hydrogen supply, and glows red. A white dwarf is the remains of a dying star that appears faint in a telescope, while a red dwarf is a slow-burning star that is smaller than our sun. Red dwarfs are the most common type of star in the Milky Way. They produce little light, so it is difficult to see them from Earth.

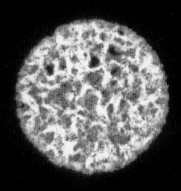

RED GIANT

RUNNING OUT OF GAS

Stars can eventually run out of their main source of fuel, hydrogen. When that happens, they undergo great changes. They may increase in size and become a red giant, running on helium instead. When that runs out, they will either begin using heavier elements as fuel or slowly cool down and die. How they die depends on how massive they are. Smaller stars cough their outer layers into space as they sputter out. Larger stars become supernovas, spewing the last of their contents into the surrounding universe in a dramatic blast of heat and fury.

PULSAR

A STAR IS BORN

Stars are born when part of a nebula—an immense cloud of gas and dust—collapses in on itself as a result of gravity. Because more gas is now squeezed into a smaller area, its gravity increases. That, in turn, increases the pressure on the gas. The tremendous pressure makes the gas cloud ignite, and a star is born.

PULSING PULSARS

Pulsars are types of stars that appear to brighten and dim at regular intervals. They are formed when the cores of massive stars compress and collapse. What causes this unusual pulsing behavior? The stars don't really change their brightness on a regular timetable. Pulsars only seem to pulse because of the way they rotate. Like a spinning light atop a lighthouse, a pulsar's beam of radiation only falls on Earth periodically. Pulsars can pulse every couple of seconds or thousands of times a second. They are so regular that they are sometimes used by astronomers as a sort of celestial timekeeper.

GALACTIC FACT ON A CLEAR NIGHT, ABOUT 3,000 STARS CAN BE VIEWED FROM EARTH WITHOUT A TELESCOPE.

A FLASH IN THE SKY

HAVE YOU EVER SEEN A

SHOOTING STAR? IF SO, YOU'VE SPOTTED one of the most fascinating objects in near space. Shooting stars aren't really stars. They are space rocks, or meteors, that burn up as they pass through Earth's atmosphere. Billions of small objects hurtle through our universe every day. Usually, they are too small or too far away to see. But every once in a while, they buzz Earth, or enter our atmosphere. They sometimes even smash into the planet!

HALLEY'S COMET

COMETS: COMING IN FROM THE COLD

Comets are small balls of rock, dust, and ice that are usually found in the darkest, coldest areas of our solar system: the Kuiper belt and the Oort cloud. The Kuiper belt is a massive loop of gases, frozen objects, asteroids, and dwarf planets far out in the solar system. The Oort cloud is a sphere-shaped cloud of icy debris on the edge of the solar system. Depending on the size and shape of their orbits, comets sometimes visit the inner parts of the solar system. The most well-known, Halley's comet, returns to the inner solar system every 76 years. Others can take thousands of years to return.

MIGHTY METEOROIDS

Shooting star, falling star, meteoroid, meteorite, meteor. It may sound confusing, but they are all different names for the same thing ... well, almost. A meteoroid is a small space rock that varies in size from a small fleck to about 3.5 feet (1.06 m) wide. As it falls through the sky at great speed, the streak of light it leaves while burning through Earth's atmosphere is called a meteor, shooting star, or falling star. If the meteoroid makes it through the atmosphere and lands on Earth, it is called a meteorite. Sometimes a group of meteoroids enter Earth's atmosphere at the same time, creating a light show called a meteor shower.

METEOR SHOWER

GALACTIC FACT COMETS HAVE TAILS OF DUST AND GAS THAT MELT AND GLOW WHEN THEY ZOOM NEAR THE SUN.

ASTOUNDING ASTEROIDS

Asteroids are leftovers from the formation of the solar system. Like meteoroids, they are space rocks, but they are much, much larger. Some asteroids are so big they could almost be considered dwarf planets, or small planetlike rocks that orbit the sun. Scientists study asteroids to gain clues as to what our solar system was like billions of years ago.

SCIENTISTS BELIEVE THAT 65 MILLION YEARS AGO AN ASTEROID ABOUT 9 MILES (15 KM) WIDE HIT THE EARTH'S SURFACE. IT WIPED OUT UP TO 90 PERCENT OF ALL LIFE ON EARTH, INCLUDING THE DINOSAURS!

ASTEROID

The asteroid Ida is shown here with its moon Dactyl. Dactyl is the first moon discovered to be orbiting an asteroid.

The sky lights up as the Chelyabinsk meteor zooms through Earth's atmosphere.

BRACE FOR IMPACT!

When you look at the moon, you can see craters on its surface. These dents are the remains of ancient smackdowns from asteroids, meteors, or comets. Crashes between space objects are not uncommon. In fact, Earth's atmosphere gets bombarded by meteors every day. The atmosphere deflects or burns up all but the largest contenders. Some, however, explode on contact. When they do, you can see, hear, and even feel it! On February 15, 2013, the Chelyabinsk meteor exploded in the sky above Russia. The light from the meteor appeared brighter than the sun, even from 62 miles (100 km) away. Eyewitnesses also reported feeling intense heat from the fireball and smelling gunpowder. It was a small meteor by impact standards, but still, the blast produced a hot cloud of dust and gas, as well as a powerful shock wave that damaged more than 7,000 buildings.

THE UNIVERSE UNFOLDS

SPACE IS SO VAST, IT'S NO SURPRISE THAT IT CONTAINS MYSTERIES

that we cannot fully understand or explain. Some space phenomena are downright freaky! Imagine, for example, a quasar—a giant column of light and radiation so intense that it is brighter than the brightest star. Or consider dark matter and dark energy—the stuff that makes up 95 percent of the universe. We can't see them, but we can detect their effects on the universe.

HEY, NOODLE LEGS!

Imagine you are being pulled into a black hole. Your body will go through a process called spaghettification. As you pass the event horizon, the part of you that enters first will experience more gravity than the part that enters last. That means the first part—say, your legs—will get pulled harder and faster than the rest of you. Your legs will stretch, streeetch, stt-r-ee-tt-ccch out like strands of interstellar spaghetti.

A BANG AND UNSEEN FORCES

First, there was the big bang—a mighty explosion that brought the universe into existence and forced it to expand. Scientists once thought that the expansion of the universe would eventually slow and stop. The universe would then collapse back in on itself and end with a big crunch. Instead, scientists now find that the universe is expanding faster, and the fuel keeping the cosmos growing is called dark energy. Dark energy is one of the magnificent mysteries of space. It makes up 70 percent of the universe but it can't be seen directly. Dark matter—another unseen substance—makes up 25 percent of the universe. Scientists know dark matter exists because of the gravitational effect it has on galaxies.

Spaghettification is a term named after spaghetti noodles.

SPIRAL GALAXY

RING GALAXY

IRREGULAR GALAXY

GALAXY SHAPES

Galaxies can come in different shapes and sizes. Spiral galaxies have a black hole at the center, with all of the stars rotating around it. Our own galaxy, the Milky Way, is a spiral galaxy. Ring galaxies, typically, are younger galaxies that have very few stars near their center. They can form after galactic collisions in which the material in the center of one galaxy gets yanked out by a larger, heavier galaxy. Like spiral galaxies, they tend to have black holes at their centers. Irregular galaxies can vary greatly in shape and, at times, have no obvious pattern.

QUASAR

QUASARS

Quasars are special types of supermassive black holes at the center of certain galaxies. They emit massive bursts of radiation, and they are the brightest, most energetic objects in existence. Quasars are created when large amounts of material are attracted to a black hole at the same time. As the material falls into the black hole, it gets heated up millions of degrees. The energy it releases can be greater than that from all the stars in the galaxy combined!

GALACTIC FACT GALAXY TYPES INCLUDE SPIRAL, RING, AND IRREGULAR.

THE SEARCH FOR LIFE

HELLO? HELLO? IS THERE

ANYONE OUT THERE? EARTHLINGS HAVE long wondered whether life exists on other planets. What if aliens live in another galaxy? Would they be like us? Could we even communicate with extraterrestrials, or would our differences make that impossible? We have so many questions but few solid answers. Yet, with research currently under way, that may change.

EARTH CALLING

In 1974, the most powerful radio signal ever produced was sent out into space. Dispatched from Arecibo, Puerto Rico, the coded Arecibo message was developed by scientists Frank Drake, Carl Sagan, and others. It was thought that the message might one day be heard by aliens. The message contained information about our knowledge of space and physics. It also contained a little bit about what humans look like and how we work.

The extraterrestrial in the movie *E.T.* had the big eyes and long neck and fingers that many Earthlings think aliens have. E.T. could also communicate telepathically.

THE ARECIBO OBSERVATORY

GALACTIC FACT THE TERM "EXTRATERRESTRIAL" MEANS "BEYOND EARTH."

LISTENING IN

In the summer of 1960, astronomer and astrophysicist Frank Drake made the first modern, scientific effort to find extraterrestrials. He scanned radio waves called microwaves coming from nearby space to see if they might contain a message, or a hint of a message. While Drake's search did not turn up anything, it encouraged other scientists to try too. The SETI Institute was formed in 1984 to research the origin and nature of life in the universe. SETI stands for Search for Extraterrestrial Intelligence. SETI explores and educates people on the search for life in the universe.

FRANK DRAKE

Frank Drake is a pioneer in extraterrestrial research. He and other scientists created the Arecibo message that was sent out by SETI in 1974 to search for extraterrestrial life.

CARL SAGAN

Astronomer and astrophysicist Carl Sagan (1934–1996) was a pioneer of exobiology, the study of the origin and evolution of life in the universe. He believed in scientific research into the possibility of life outside of our planet. Sagan was also a NASA adviser, working with astronauts and contributing to robotic mission experiments. He put together the first physical message sent into space—on golden records attached to several NASA space probes.

LITTLE GREEN MEN?

We can only imagine what aliens might look like. And boy, have we imagined! From science-fiction books to blockbuster movies, aliens have looked a lot like humans with two arms, legs, eyes, and ears—although those arms might have been green and the aliens 4 feet (1.2 m) tall. If aliens exist, they might not look like humans at all! Most astrobiologists—scientists who explore the possibility of life in space—think the likeliest form of life there would be microbes, such as bacteria or viruses.

EXPLORER'S CORNER

Did you know that you can help look for alien life? With the help of a teacher, parent, or friend, you can install special software that lets your computer scan radio data taken by astronomical observatories for signals from an extraterrestrial civilization. Search the Internet for "SETI@home" and give it a shot! Personally, I study distant galaxies and their weird shapes, but I also help other astronomers look for aliens. It's a lot of fun, and you never know what you might find!

A PHOTO GALLERY

OUT OF THIS WORLD!

HOW'S THE VIEW
UP THERE? WHETHER
looking up from Earth, through a telescope, or down from a space station, the views of and from space are incredible. Earth appears as a big blue marble, and distant galaxies, seen pictured from high-powered telescopes, look like fantastic creatures.

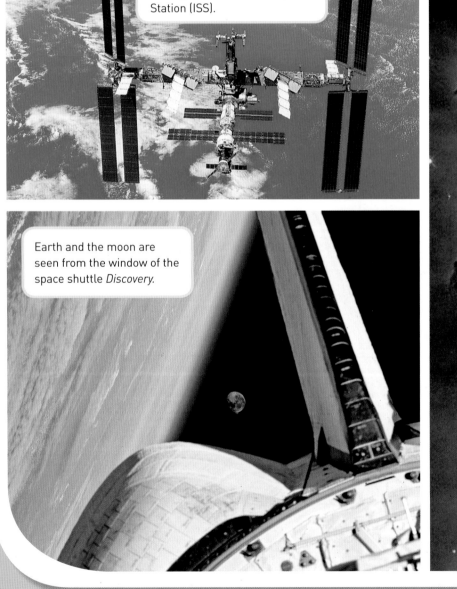

With Earth as a background, the space shuttle *Atlantis* is shown leaving the International Space Station (ISS).

Earth and the moon are seen from the window of the space shuttle *Discovery*.

A star cluster lights up a giant cloud of gas in this telescope image.

An image of Hurricane Isabel, taken from the International Space Station, shows the calm blue eye of the storm and its enormous circulating cloud cover.

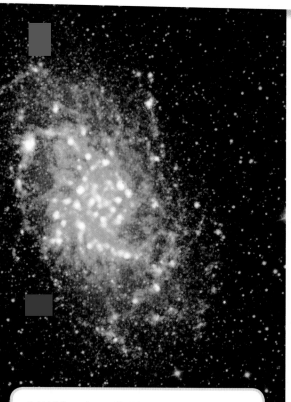

A NASA probe took this image of one of the Milky Way's closest neighboring galaxies, Messier 33, or Triangulum.

From space, Earth's weather systems, oceans, and landmasses seem as though they were taken from a giant painting.

THE FINAL
FRONTIER

An artist's illustration of Mars, the red planet, showing a robotic rover exploring the planet's surface, with a comet visible in the sky above, passing beyond the planet.

THE SPACE RACE

NOT SO LONG AGO, HUMANS COULD

ONLY DREAM OF SPACEFLIGHT, AND WALKING ON THE moon was a fantasy. Only in the past century have we had the technology to reach beyond our planet. Once humans had the ability to go beyond the bounds of Earth, space became so compelling that two of the world's greatest powers competed to put the first humans in space and on the moon. From 1955 to 1972, a rivalry called the "space race" pitted the United States against the (now former) Union of Soviet Socialist Republics, or U.S.S.R., in a quest for space supremacy.

SPUTNIK SATELLITE

Satellites are space objects that orbit Earth, such as the moon. Artificial satellites are objects that orbit Earth and are used for communications, weather monitoring, or navigation. The world's first artificial satellite was launched by the former Soviet Union on October 4, 1957. Sputnik 1 was about the size of a beach ball and contained scientific equipment to gather data. Its launch kicked off the space race.

SPACE DOG HERO

Before a human could be launched into space, we had to find out if would be safe. Test animals were sent into space as the world's first astronauts and cosmonauts. First, monkeys and mice were sent up in rockets. Then, in 1957 the Soviet Union sent a dog named Laika into space on orbiting spacecraft Sputnik 2. When monkeys and dogs sent into space in the late 1950s and early 1960s came back alive, it proved that it was possible to survive in space.

LAIKA IN SPUTNIK 2

FIRST MOONWALK

Both the U.S. and U.S.S.R. vied to be the first to reach the moon. The U.S.S.R. got there first, with an unmanned lander called Lunik 2, in 1959. The U.S. space program, run by the National Aeronautics and Space Administration (NASA), named their lunar exploration program Apollo, after the Roman sun god. On July 20, 1969, American astronaut Neil Armstrong became the first human to walk on the moon. As he stepped on lunar soil, he uttered this famous line: "That's one small step for man, one giant leap for mankind." In that landmark mission, astronaut Buzz Aldrin also walked on the moon. Since then, 21 other astronauts, all Americans, have made it to the moon, and 12 have walked on its surface.

SPACE RACE FIRSTS

OCT. 4, 1957
- Sputnik 1 launches.

NOV. 3, 1957
- Sputnik 2 launches with Laika on board.

JAN. 31, 1958
- Explorer 1, the first U.S. satellite, detects radiation belts.

APR. 12, 1961
- Yuri Gagarin becomes the first human in space.

JUNE 16, 1963
- Vostok 6 launches with the first woman in space, Valentina Tereshkova.

GALACTIC FACT   THE APOLLO MISSIONS EACH TOOK ABOUT THREE DAYS TO REACH THE MOON.

BUZZ ALDRIN
ON THE MOON

NEIL ARMSTRONG

HUMANS IN SPACE

Of all the possible world records and "firsts," the title of first human in space is a big one. That title goes to Soviet cosmonaut Yuri Gagarin. In 1961, the Soviet Union launched Gagarin in the Vostok 1 spacecraft. Gagarin orbited Earth, reentered the atmosphere, and landed safely. Also in 1961, astronaut Alan Shepard became the first American to travel in space, aboard Freedom 7, while John Glenn became the first American to orbit Earth, aboard Friendship 7.

JOHN GLENN BOARDING
FRIENDSHIP 7

The space shuttle *Challenger* exploded less than two minutes after liftoff in 1986. Seven crew members died.

YURI GAGARIN
ABOARD VOSTOK 1

SPACE TRAGEDY

Space can be a dangerous place, and the space race and space exploration has claimed many lives. A Soviet launchpad accident in 1960 killed an estimated 100 scientists and military personnel gathered for the launch of a test rocket. Called the Nedelin catastrophe, it was one of the earliest space disasters. Dozens of astronauts and cosmonauts have died either trying to get to space or on the way back. Vladimir Komarov was the first Soviet cosmonaut killed, when his capsule, Soyuz I, failed to deploy its parachute in 1967. In that same year, the three-member American crew of Apollo 1—Virgil "Gus" Grissom, Roger Chaffee, and Edward White—died in a fire during a launch simulation. The space shuttle program has had its share of tragedy too. The shuttle *Columbia* broke apart as it returned to Earth after a two-week mission in 2003. Seven crew members were lost in that accident.

JULY 20, 1969
- Apollo 11 mission brings the first humans to walk on the moon.

APR. 19, 1971
- Salyut 1, the first human-crewed space station, launches.

NOV. 13, 1971
- Mariner 9 becomes the first spacecraft to orbit Mars.

JULY 15, 1972
- Pioneer 10, the first space mission to leave the inner solar system, enters the asteroid belt.

JULY 15, 1975
- Apollo-Soyuz Test Project—the first multinational human-crewed space mission—launches.

INFINITY AND BEYOND

IN THE MOVIES, SPACE

TRAVELERS JUMP FROM EARTH TO the outer reaches of the galaxy covering billions of space miles in minutes, thanks to hyperdrive spaceships. They travel for months or years living in a kind of hibernation called stasis. And when they emerge, they walk out of their space pods as if they are walking on air. Humans dream of easy space travel, but we are a long way from exploring the galaxy in starships.

PROBING SPACE

What do you do when you want to learn more about space but don't have the ability to send human space explorers? You send robotic probes! These probes are sent to explore and study space. Space agencies also launch artificial satellites to study Earth and help us communicate, navigate, and monitor the planet's weather. Space probes and research satellites do experiments remotely, without any people on board. Probes can be sent to distant destinations that take months or years to reach, while satellites orbit Earth, delivering a steady stream of data.

SPACESHIPS OF THE **FUTURE** MAY CAPTURE THE **SUN'S POWER,** USING **SOLAR SAILS** TO REACH **SPEEDS** OF **56 MILES PER SECOND** (90 KM/S).

TO THE MOON, AGAIN

No human has set foot on the moon since NASA's Apollo 17 astronauts in 1972. But it's likely that someone will go there again, soon. China has launched an ambitious lunar exploration program in which probes have mapped the moon in 3-D, and rovers have explored its surface. The moon has deposits of titanium and other metals that might make it valuable for mining in the future. If space travel becomes easier and more affordable, Earthlings could some day live and work on the moon.

The lunar rover used on NASA's Apollo missions was called the "moon buggy" because it looked like the dune buggy vehicles used on Earth at the time to travel over sand dunes.

GALACTIC FACT   THE VOYAGER 1 PROBE IS SO FAR FROM EARTH, IT TAKES 17 HOURS TO RECEIVE OR SEND A MESSAGE!

SPACE STATIONS

Seeing what's out there is just one part of space exploration. Scientists also want to know how space works. To find out, they design and perform experiments in space station labs. Space stations are Earth-orbiting research labs where scientists can remain in space, conducting experiments while living there for months at a time. Many of the experiments study the effects of long-term spaceflight to see if humans really can live in space. The International Space Station is the most well-known space station. It has been under continuous construction since 1998.

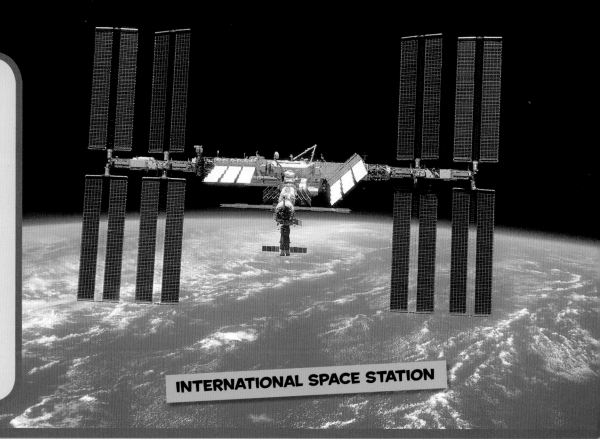

INTERNATIONAL SPACE STATION

SPACE TOURISM

How's this for a trip of a lifetime? If you've got the money, a number of private space travel companies are now offering trips to space. The first flights into space for nonprofessional astronauts cost from $95,000 to $250,000 for a few hours in the outer reaches of Earth's atmosphere. Tourists are required to attend two-to-three-day training sessions on spaceflight and zero-gravity environments.

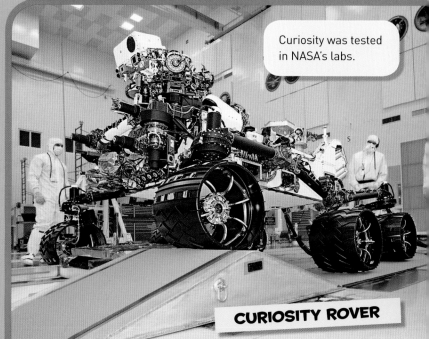

Curiosity was tested in NASA's labs.

CURIOSITY ROVER

MARS HOTEL

Space tourism companies may one day offer vacations at hotels on the moon or Mars.

LIFE ON MARS?

NASA's Curiosity rover launched in 2011 and landed on the surface of Mars about a year and a half later. The car-size robot is searching for signs of life and water on the red planet. It is also studying the soil and rocks of Mars. So far it has discovered that Mars may have once had conditions that suited bacterial life.

SPACE STATIONS

WITH THE RIGHT PREPARATION, HUMANS CAN AND DO SAFELY LIVE AND WORK IN SPACE. LIFE IS DIFFERENT UP THERE THAN IT IS

on Earth. And one of the biggest differences is that you get a far better view!

NO WALK IN THE PARK

Make no mistake, spaceflight is risky. There is no guarantee that an astronaut who goes up can make it home safely. But the risk has been reduced since the 1960s. Still, launching even small spacecraft into orbit requires megalift. The earliest rockets relied on additional boosters and thrusters to provide enough power to escape Earth's atmosphere. Each would ignite at a different time to add *oomph* to the rocket's trajectory. The boosters would then fall off during different stages of liftoff. When a craft returned to Earth, much of the ride would be left behind. Reentry into Earth's atmosphere caused so much friction that only the smallest spacecraft could survive it, leaving a stripped-down reentry vehicle to splash down in the ocean for a warm, wet reception.

SHUTTLE AND SPACE STATIONS

The United States developed the space shuttle in 1981. Its great advantage over earlier spacecraft was that it could be reused. That greatly reduced the cost of space travel. The shuttle had small living compartments for the crew and a larger compartment to transport satellites and satellite repair modules. The first space station was launched by the Soviet Union in component parts from 1971 to 1986. The U.S. launched its first in 1973, and the International Space Station (ISS) was first launched in component parts in 1998. Dozens of astronauts and scientists have visited these floating space laboratories for weeks or months at a time.

SPACE SUITS HIDE A PATCH OF VELCRO IN THE HELMET SO ASTRONAUTS CAN SCRATCH THEIR NOSES!

GALACTIC FACT CHINA LAUNCHED ITS FIRST SPACE STATION IN 2011.

LIVING IN SPACE

Movies and television shows depict living in space as something like living on Earth. Space inhabitants are shown walking easily through halls, eating fresh foods, and looking fit and muscular. But in reality, living in space is no easy feat. Astronauts who live in space have to live in zero-gravity conditions for long periods of time. That takes its toll on their bodies. Without gravity, bones and muscles gradually lose mass. To prevent this from happening, astronauts aboard the ISS must exercise regularly. Even though astronauts use special exercise equipment, when they return to Earth their muscles are weak and take time to adjust to the planet's gravity. But zero g isn't all bad. On Earth gravity tugs on your eyeballs, changing their shape. The bigger the shape change, the greater the vision change. Some ISS astronauts have reported better distance vision after spending months in space at zero g.

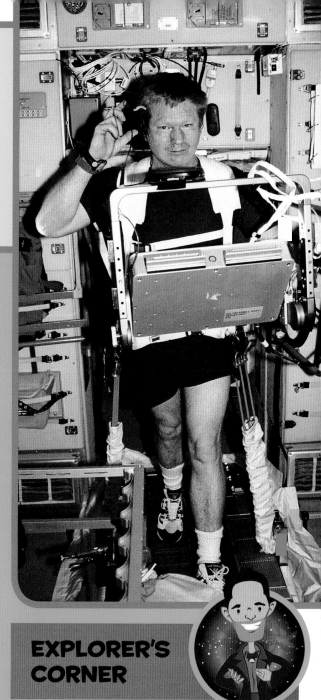

SCRUB-A-DUB

Keeping fresh is difficult for astronauts. Elbow room is limited and water is in short supply. Astronauts are only allowed a few drops a day for brushing their teeth or washing their faces. When they're really stinky, astronauts can opt for a sponge bath, using a single squeeze of water, or they can take a quick shower in a barely-there stall. When they're done, they use a vacuum to suck off any remaining water. Space stations have special toilets that suck away waste too! When astronauts go on space walks, they wear maximum absorption garments, or MAGs, inside their space suits. These are special diapers that ensure they don't have any accidents out in space.

EXPLORER'S CORNER

Being an astronaut sounds tough, doesn't it? The difficulties of living in space are made worse by the fact that it takes a long time to get anywhere in the universe. When leaving Earth, astronauts travel 6.8 miles per second (11 km/s)! If you were an astronaut and kept going at that speed, you would zoom by the moon in about ten hours, and pass by the sun in about five months. To reach Neptune and the outskirts of the solar system, it would take you 13 years! What about the nearest stars? Try 117,000 years. The other side of our galaxy? That would take two billion years!

FREEZE-DRIED ICE CREAM, ANYONE?

Suppertime in space is a delicate operation. Cooking is impossible when your pot floats around the room. So astronauts eat mostly prepared foods such as macaroni and cheese, scrambled eggs, and chicken. That's a far cry from the freeze-dried powders astronauts ate in the 1960s. But most foods still come dehydrated, in sealed bags. Astronauts add water to them before they are eaten. A spill would be disastrous because the crumbs and liquid could damage sensitive equipment. To keep everyone safe, all liquids must be sipped through a straw from a sealed bag. All astronauts must also be members of the "clean plate club." They have to eat every bit of their food, because no leftovers are allowed.

ASTRONAUT ICE CREAM

SPACE HEROES

THOUSANDS OF SCIENTISTS, ASTRONAUTS, AND COSMONAUTS HAVE DEDICATED THEIR LIVES TO IMPROVING OUR UNDERSTANDING

of space. Some of these heroes of outer space risked their reputations and their lives studying what's out there and daring to travel beyond the bounds of Earth.

U.S.S.R.—ENGINEER, COSMONAUT
MARCH 6, 1937–

Tereshkova was a factory worker whose fearlessness and skydiving skills earned her an opportunity to join the Soviet space program. She became the first woman in space on June 16, 1963, when she was launched in the Soviet Vostok 6 spacecraft. She spent three days orbiting Earth. Later, she earned a doctorate in engineering.

VALENTINA TERESHKOVA

U.S.A.—DOCTOR, ENGINEER, ASTRONAUT
OCTOBER 17, 1956–

At age 16, Jemison attended Stanford University, where she earned a degree in chemical engineering, before going on to medical school and becoming a doctor. As a child, she always believed she would be an astronaut. She became the first African-American woman in space when she worked as a scientist conducting experiments in weightlessness and motion sickness during her eight days orbiting in the space shuttle *Endeavour* in 1992.

MAE JEMISON

VALERI POLYAKOV

RUSSIA—COSMONAUT, DOCTOR
APRIL 27, 1942–

Polyakov set a record for spending 437 days in space aboard the space station Mir in 1994–1995. He spent those days doing medical research on long-term spaceflight to help us better understand how to live in space. The first person to spend more than a year in space, Polyakov traveled more than 186 million miles (299 million km) and orbited the earth 7,075 times.

GALACTIC FACT   ASTRONAUT ALAN SHEPARD HIT A GOLF BALL ON THE MOON IN 1971.

JOHN GLENN

U.S.A.—PILOT, ENGINEER, ASTRONAUT
JULY 18, 1921–

Glenn became the first American to orbit Earth when he flew the Friendship 7 in 1962. A fighter pilot who served in World War II and the Korean War, Glenn later became a test pilot before joining NASA. He received a ticker-tape parade after his orbit of Earth.

CHRIS HADFIELD

CANADA—PILOT, ENGINEER, ASTRONAUT
AUGUST 29, 1959–

Hadfield became known as the singing astronaut after taking his guitar to the International Space Station and sharing songs on social media during a mission he commanded in 2013. Hadfield flew in space three times and was the first Canadian to walk in space.

LIU YANG

CHINA—PILOT, ASTRONAUT
OCTOBER 6, 1978–

China's first female astronaut, or *taikonaut*, Liu Yang was a transport pilot before launching aboard Shenzou 9 in 2012. She traveled to Chinese space station Tiangong 1 exactly 49 years to the day after the world's first female cosmonaut, Valentina Tereshkova, made her historic spaceflight.

SPACE COMPARISONS

THE ANCIENT

PEOPLES OF EARTH STUDIED the sky. Unknowingly, they were observing space too! Since they lacked the sophisticated tools that we have now, they sometimes made mistakes. Today, we know precisely which best guesses about space were nothing but best messes. Here are some examples of ancient ideas that don't mesh with our modern understanding of space.

WHAT ORBITS WHAT?

NOW: We know that only the moon and our artificial satellites orbit Earth.

THEN: Most ancient astronomers thought that Earth was the center of the universe. They thought everything—the sun, the moon, the stars— orbited Earth.

ROUND IS SOUND?

THEN: The ancients believed that the planets and the moons were divine. As a result, they must have perfectly round orbits to reflect their godliness.

NOW: We know that most orbits are elliptical, closer to ovals than perfect circles.

MAN IN THE MOON

THEN: People once thought that other people or other beings inhabited the moon, the stars, or Mars.

NOW: While we know life on other worlds is a very real possibility, so far no signs of life have been found in the solar system or galaxy beyond.

STARS VS. SUN

THEN: People thought our sun was unique and there was nothing else like it. It had nothing to do with the stars in the sky.

NOW: We know that stars like our sun are common, but dimmer and redder stars are more common.

ASTROLOGY

NOW: Skip your daily horoscope. Astrology has now been thoroughly debunked. The heavens have no provable direct impact on an individual's life.

THEN: Mystics once used the positions of the stars to attempt to predict events on Earth or in a person's life. If Venus was in a particular position relative to the moon, for example, it could mean that you were going to fall in love, or get a cold.

4 SPACE FUN

Russian astronauts put Chinese space tourists through zero-gravity flight training exercises at the Yuri A. Gagarin Research and Test Cosmonaut Training Center in Moscow. The exercises let the tourists feel what it is like to float around in a space station.

ARE YOU AN ASTRONAUT OR AN ASTRONOMER?

IOW THAT YOU KNOW EVERYTHING ABOUT SPACE,

YOU'RE READY TO GO OUT AND EXPLORE THE STILL UNDISCOVERED CORNERS OF

the universe, right? But there are so many different jobs out there. Which space career would suit you best? Take this out-of-this-world quiz and find out which career will leave you starstruck.

1 What's your favorite thing to do on the weekend?

A. Play brainteaser games, such as Clue or Risk
B. Play video games for hours on end
C. Play a team sport, such as soccer or hockey
D. Get your buddies together and go play laser tag
E. Watch a movie, read a book, or write a story

2 Feeling blue? What do you do to dunk the funk?

A. Think through what's bothering you, and then solve the problem and move on
B. Build something out of Legos or tinker with a bicycle
C. Hang out with a friend
D. Go for a run
E. Write in your journal

3 What's your favorite class in school?

A. Science
B. Industrial Arts
C. Math
D. Gym
E. English

4. Your ideal family vacation would be:

A. Visiting NASA headquarters
B. Going to a science center where you can build robots
C. It doesn't matter, as long as you get to pick the destination and plan the trip
D. Going to an amusement park—you're crazy about roller coasters
E. Staying home and indulging in a movie marathon

5 What words best describe you?

A. Clever
B. Problem Solver
C. Team Player
D. Adventurous
E. Dreamer

6 If school were closed for a day, what would you do?

A. Go to the library and read all you can about math, science, and how the universe works
B. Build your own space station from household materials
C. Plan a space-oriented event and organize every activity down to the minute
D. Hang upside down from a tree while reading a book about space exploration
E. Interview your friends and write a story about them

WHAT'S YOUR IDEAL SPACE CAREER?

IF YOU SCORED MOSTLY

A's: You would make a great **astronomer** or **astrophysicist.** You have a sharp mind and plenty of curiosity. Your mission in life is to discover how things work. As a researcher studying space, you will have endless opportunities to explore your passions—there is a whole universe out there to discover!

IF YOU SCORED MOSTLY

C's: You would excel as a **mission controller!** You've got the goods for leading a team and overseeing all aspects of a space exploration mission. You'll be at the head of the team, with your feet on the ground, and your decisions will guide the whole process from start to finish. It's good to be the boss.

IF YOU SCORED MOSTLY

D's: You would do great as an **astronaut.** You're the kind of person who needs to get out there, wherever "there" is! You have boundless energy and love to work with people. You're also daring, and up for adventure—at any time, any place. You're fit both mentally and physically—with a mind that enjoys all aspects of science and exploration.

IF YOU SCORED MOSTLY

E's: You'd enjoy being a **journalist** reporting about space. Although it would be nice to report from space, that is not yet a possibility. Space journalists travel to launch and training sites, but they do a lot of research from the office too. You'll get to talk to people and learn new information from firsthand accounts, online research, and scientific journals.

ROCKET ENGINEER

MISSION CONTROLLER

ASTRONOMER

ASTRONAUT

GALACTIC FACT AMATEUR ASTRONOMERS HAVE DISCOVERED STARS AND PLANETS ORBITING DOUBLE STARS.

STARGAZING

YOU DON'T HAVE TO BE AN ASTRONOMER TO STUDY
THE NIGHT SKY. EVEN WITHOUT A TELESCOPE, YOU CAN WATCH AWESOME SKY THEATER
from your own backyard, although your viewing will be much better in a dark area, away from the light pollution of a city.

AURORA BOREALIS

CURTAINS OF COLOR

The aurora borealis, or northern lights, is a phenomenon that occurs in northern areas, such as Alaska, U.S.A., and northern Canada. Streamers of light fill the sky, captivating all who witness them. They are caused by charged particles from the sun becoming trapped in the magnetic atmosphere close to our planet's poles. The aurora australis provides the same type of light show for the Southern Hemisphere.

ISS

SHOOTING STAR OR PASSING SATELLITE?

Is it a star? A planet? Or a comet? Tick off "none of the above." Satellites and space stations can be seen whipping across the night sky too! They look like fast-moving dots of light. The ISS is best seen before dawn and before dusk as a slow-moving point of light. It takes ten minutes for it to cross from horizon to horizon.

GALACTIC FACT THE MILKY WAY IS SO BIG THAT IT TAKES LIGHT 100,000 YEARS TO CROSS FROM ONE SIDE TO THE OTHER.

VENUS

EVENING STAR

Venus is sometimes called the Evening Star because it appears at its brightest shortly before the sun sets. It's very bright right before dawn too!

MAPS OF THE STARS

A star chart is like a road map to the stars. You can buy star charts or download them from the Internet to match and identify stars. Here are some handy tips on how to use them:

CHOOSE A CLEAR NIGHT, WHEN THERE'S LITTLE OR NO CLOUD COVER.

GET THE CORRECT CHART. THE CHARTS SOMETIMES CHANGE MONTHLY TO MATCH WHAT APPEARS IN THE SKY.

FIND OUT WHAT DIRECTION YOU ARE FACING AND USE A QUARTER OF THE MAP WITH SOME OF THE BRIGHTEST CONSTELLATIONS ON IT.

LOOK UP AND SEARCH FOR THE IMAGE YOU SAW ON THE CHART. CHOOSE ONE CONSTELLATION AND GO FROM THERE.

WRITTEN IN THE STARS

On a clear night you should be able to see several groups of stars, or constellations, in the sky. Become a star-watcher and match these constellation descriptions with their image.

A HERCULES

1 The brightest star in the night sky, Sirius, is found in this dog-shaped constellation. It's only visible in the Southern Hemisphere.

B CASSIOPEIA

2 This 15-star constellation bears the Latin name for "dragon." Its "tail" winds between the Big and Little Dippers.

C URSA MAJOR

3 This squarish constellation is named for a superstrong mythological hero. Can you see his muscular arms and legs?

4 The well-known Great Bear constellation is visible in the Northern Hemisphere. Its seven brightest stars form what is called the Big Dipper, or the Plow.

D CANIS MAJOR

5 Sometimes called the Queen, this constellation resembles either an M or a W, depending on the time of year. It's named for a queen who boasted she was more beautiful than the nymphs of the sea.

E DRACO

ANSWERS: 1. d; 2. e; 3. a; 4. c; 5. b

FACT VS. MYTH

THINK YOU ARE AN

EXPERT ON SPACE? WANT TO TEST YOUR knowledge of the vast unknown? Which of these popular ideas about space are facts, and which are myths?

A THE SUN IS A FIERY BALL OF GASES.

B ASTEROID BELTS, LIKE THE ONE IN OUR SOLAR SYSTEM, ARE DIFFICULT TO NAVIGATE AND ARE FULL OF DEADLY SPACE ROCKS.

C GRAVITY IS THE FORCE THAT CAUSES ALL THINGS, INCLUDING BEAMS OF LIGHT, TO BE ATTRACTED TO EACH OTHER.

D ASTRONAUTS IN SPACE HAVE TO WEAR DIAPERS.

E THE FASTER YOU MOVE, THE SLOWER TIME PASSES.

A. MYTH
The sun does not burn; it glows from the intense heat. It is too hot for flames to form!

GALACTIC FACT SINCE GRAVITY AFFECTS TIME, YOUR FEET AGE SLIGHTLY FASTER THAN YOUR HEAD.

C. FACT

Gravity has the ability to warp space, affecting the path of objects and even light. Scientists watch how light bends as a way to help them indirectly detect dark matter and weigh galaxies.

B. MYTH

Space is so big that even asteroid belts are relatively empty. When a probe is sent through the asteroid belt, the possibility of hitting a space rock is so remote, scientists barely consider it!

D. FACT

Space diapers are called Maximum Absorption Garments (MAGs) and must be worn inside a space suit. They are also worn during the takeoff and landing of spacecraft. Inside the space shuttle quarters, astronauts use a special toilet when they've got to go.

E. FACT

Speed and gravity directly affect how an object experiences time. The faster you go, the slower time will pass for you compared to slower objects. Taking this into account, satellites orbiting Earth have their clocks set at a deliberately slower pace than clocks on Earth.

SPACE AND CULTURE

SCARY INSECTLIKE ALIENS, POWERFUL
TALKING COMPUTERS THAT TAKE CONTROL OF SPACESHIPS, AND

evil intergalactic empires—they've all been in stories imagined and told in science-fiction movies, television shows, and books. Space captures the imagination in a way that few other subjects have or can. Perhaps that's why we can't get enough of it.

COOL TOOLS:
SCI-FI FANTASY MADE REAL

Fantastic gadgets and cool tech have always been a popular feature of space-based film and TV. They made people dream of owning futuristic devices such as personal communicators or flying cars. Some wound up inspiring real-life innovations.

MATCH THESE INVENTIONS WITH THEIR FANTASY INSPIRATION:

1 CELL PHONES   **2** TWIN ION ENGINES

3 AIRCAR   **4** SUPERPOWERED FLASHLIGHT   **5** SIRI

A

THE JETSONS' FLYING CAR

Cartoon character George Jetson had a flying car that inspired Milner Motors to develop their airborne vehicle. It should be available on the market soon—for highfliers flaunting plenty of cash.

B

VOICE-ACTIVATED COMPUTER

In *Star Trek: The Next Generation*, Captain Picard famously ordered "Tea. Earl Grey. Hot." from a knowledgeable, capable computer. The onboard computer could also answer tricky questions and perform complicated tasks on command. A voice-activated personal assistant now available in some cell phones can answer questions and plot map routes. It can't make tea yet, though.

GALACTIC FACT   COMPUTER LANGUAGE TRANSLATORS LIKE THE ONES USED IN *STAR TREK* MAY SOON EXIST IN REAL LIFE.

ANSWERS: 1. c; 2. e; 3. a; 4. d; 5. b

These devices were inspired by the communicators used in the 1960s-era TV show *Star Trek*. Communicators were small handheld objects that allowed instant two-way communication.

C

STAR TREK COMMUNICATOR

D

LIGHT SABERS

A Dutch engineer has invented a superpowered flashlight with a beam so powerful it can burn human flesh! Don't plan on getting into a light saber duel, though. To date, only a single proto-type has been produced.

TIE FIGHTERS

E

In the movie *Star Wars*, these imaginary engines powered the TIE Fighters. In reality, a similar technology has been used by space probes for more than 15 years.

DON'T CALL YOUR TRAVEL AGENT ... YET

Some fantasy space places seem so real, you want to book a visit yesterday. Some sci-fi inventions are also out of this world! Check out these real-world comparisons:

FANTASY:
In *Star Wars*, Luke Skywalker hails from Tatooine, a desert world lit by two suns.

REALITY:
Astronomers have identified several planets that orbit two stars.

FANTASY:
In Roald Dahl's book *Charlie and the Great Glass Elevator*, Charlie and his family travel to space and stay in a space hotel for the rich and famous.

REALITY:
Virgin Galactic's SpaceShipTwo is planning to take space tourists into orbit for a fee of $212,000! SpaceX, another private space exploration company, is currently developing inflatable habitats to be used as hotels on Mars.

FANTASY:
Tractor beams can pull distant objects toward you and hold them fast! The idea originated in E. E. Smith's 1931 novel *Spacehounds of IPC*. It later appeared in Buck Rogers comic strips, *Star Trek*, *Star Wars*, *Transformers: Beast Wars*, and *The Incredibles*.

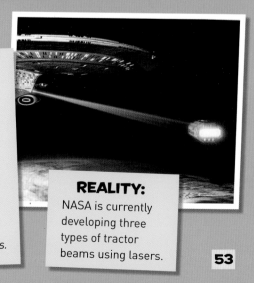

REALITY:
NASA is currently developing three types of tractor beams using lasers.

BEHIND THE SHOT WITH BRENDAN MULLAN

WILL WE EVER MEET ALIENS
FROM OTHER PLANETS? MAYBE. BUT MAYBE NOT.

Astronomy is a science. That means it uses numbers and math to prove ideas about the universe and the possibility of life on other planets. A lot of these numbers can be very big—we're talking in terms of millions, billions, and even trillions. It's often hard to think about what these numbers really mean. But here's something to think about. You know it would take astronauts a long time to traverse the space between the stars. Many people think that, within another generation, we could build better rockets and send people into space faster. Even then, it would take us about 100 million years to reach all the stars in the Milky Way galaxy—if we really worked at it, that is. That's a long time!

Imagine representing a year of time with a sheet of toilet paper. A hundred million sheets would give you enough rolls of toilet paper to fill a whole tennis court more than 6.5 feet (2 m) deep! Now consider this: The solar system is 4.6 billion years old. If years were sheets of toilet paper, there would be enough rolls of it to fill a big soccer stadium—again more than 6.5 feet (2 m) deep. And the Milky Way galaxy has had stars like our sun and planets like Earth in it for at least another soccer stadium's worth of toilet-paper time! So traveling between stars would take a very long time, yet many people think aliens do it easily and often.

The Milky Way has 400 billion stars. At least one of them should have a planet around it that supports intelligent life. That life has had more than enough time to reach us. So what's the deal? Are we alone? If so, why? Are we being left alone for some reason? Again, why? Are we the first? Are there life-forms out there who are more advanced or less advanced than us? And no, UFOs aren't real. Scientists all agree that they're hoaxes or can be explained by natural phenomena. There is absolutely no evidence that aliens have set foot on our planet. So where is everybody? What do you think?

In science-fiction books and movies, alien worlds are inhabited by creatures far more scientifically advanced than humans. But what are the chances that these worlds exist? If you ask astronomers, the answer is "not very likely." Even if they did, we are not likely to reach them, as travel to distant galaxies would take too much time.

AFTERWORD

NASA astronaut Bruce McCandless II manipulates a maneuvering unit in space on the first ever untethered space walk from a shuttle.

THINKING ABOUT SPACE STRETCHES

OUR MINDS TO IMPOSSIBLE PLACES: GIANT PLANETS

made of gas and ice, black holes that swallow entire solar systems, stars that explode in cataclysmic supernovas. It connects us to our ancestors, who gazed at the stars and saw gods at work and play. It also connects us to each other. Not only does all life on Earth owe its existence to the sun, our nearest star, but we are all made out of the same raw materials—stardust.

The more we learn about space, the more mysteries we uncover. These, in turn, compel us to search farther and dig deeper for answers. As a result, our research into space has yielded many new technologies that are useful right here on Earth. GPS satellites, accurate weather forecasts, and advanced microchip computing all grew directly from space research.

One day, maybe in your own lifetime, people will be living and working in space on a regular basis. Perhaps you will travel to work on an expanded space station like the ISS, or to a self-contained, Earthlike habitat on the moon or Mars. What will life in space be like? Only time will tell.

SPACE: THE ETERNAL FRONTIER

Our knowledge of space—what's out there, and whether it's possible to live on other planets—increases every year. The ongoing research on and exploration of space, through satellites, rockets, space stations, and probes, helps us understand how the universe works. Space researchers have successfully placed a lander on the surface of Comet 67P and rovers on Mars. The information sent back to Earth from these robotic devices may tell us how comets helped form the universe and whether there ever was life on Mars.

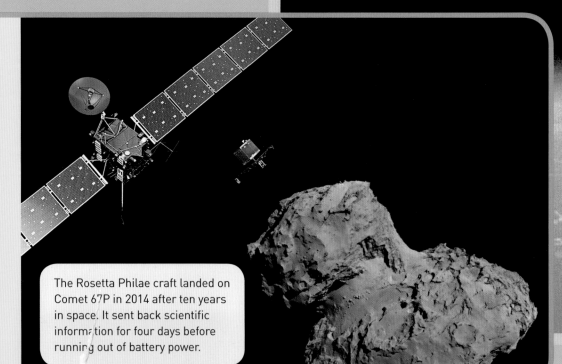

The Rosetta Philae craft landed on Comet 67P in 2014 after ten years in space. It sent back scientific information for four days before running out of battery power.

The space shuttle *Atlantis* in an image taken from above on the International Space Station (ISS). The *Atlantis* has undocked from an eight-day mission to the ISS and is returning to Earth with astronauts aboard.

AN INTERACTIVE GLOSSARY

SPACE SPEAK

Apollo 11 astronaut Buzz Aldrin takes his first step onto the surface of the moon in July 1969. Aldrin was part of the historic mission along with Neil Armstrong and Michael Collins.

ACE YOUR SPACE VOCABULARY! ARE YOU BLASTOFF
READY TO DISCOVER WORDS AND MEANINGS? READ THE GLOSSARY TO LEARN WHAT

each word means and visit the page numbers listed to see the word used in context. Then test your space knowledge!

1. Asteroid
A large rock floating in space, often in groups or belts
(PAGES 12, 13, 24, 25, 35, 50, 51)

In our solar system, where is the asteroid belt located?

a. between the sun and Mercury

b. between Mars and Jupiter

c. between Venus and Earth

d. between Saturn and Venus

2. Astronaut
People who travel to space aboard spacecraft. Russian astronauts are called cosmonauts.
(PAGES 11, 34–41, 46–47, 50, 51, 54, 56–57, 58–59, 60)

Who was the first man in space?

a. Neil Armstrong

b. Buzz Aldrin

c. Yuri Gagarin

d. Alan Shepard

3. Black Hole
The remnant of a large star that is so heavy, it pulls everything into it
(PAGES 7, 15, 19, 26, 27, 56)

What can escape a black hole's pull?

a. light

b. sound

c. nothing

d. a really fast spaceship

4. Extraterrestrial
A living being that does not come from Earth
(PAGES 14, 28–29)

What was the first message sent to extraterrestrials?

a. the Arecibo message

b. the Ariba message

c. hello!

d. E.T. phone home

5. Galaxy
A large group of stars held together by gravity
(PAGES 6–9, 11, 15–19, 22–23, 27, 29, 31, 36, 39, 43, 51, 54)

What is the name of our galaxy?

a. Pinwheel galaxy

b. Andromeda

c. Ursa Major

d. Milky Way

6. Hydrogen
An element that is the primary source of fuel for stars
(PAGES 22, 23)

When stars run out of hydrogen, they turn into what?

a. pulsars

b. red giants

c. white dwarfs

d. black holes

7. Observatory
A building with telescopes where scientists study space
(PAGES 14–15, 28, 29)

Which observatory was founded by King Charles II?

a. the Royal Observatory

b. SALT

c. the IceCube Observatory

d. ALMA

8. Rocket
A vehicle that uses a powerful engine to thrust it into air or launch a spacecraft at great speed
(PAGES 34–35, 38, 46, 47, 54, 56)

Which mission and rocket engines took the first men to the moon?

a. Vostok 1 (Vostok -k rocket)

b. Gemini 7 (Titan II GLV)

c. Soyuz IV (Soyuz)

d. Apollo 11 (Saturn V)

9. Satellite
An object that orbits a much larger object in space
(PAGES 10, 13, 34, 36, 38, 42, 48, 51, 56)

What was the name of the first human-made satellite?

a. Galileo

b. Kepler

c. Sputnik

d. Columbus

10. Spaghettification
The process by which objects pulled into a black hole get stretched out like spaghetti
(PAGE 26)

What do objects experience more of as they pass through the event horizon?

a. solar winds

b. heat

c. gravity

d. swirling

11. Space Shuttle
A type of reusable spacecraft developed by NASA
(PAGES 5, 30, 35, 38, 40, 51, 58–59)

What was the advantage of space shuttles over earlier spacecraft?

a. they could go faster

b. they could be reused

c. they could fly straight up

d. they used less fuel

12. Telescope
A tool that magnifies distant objects
(PAGES 7, 14–15, 17, 23, 30, 48)

What is the largest ground-based telescope in the Southern Hemisphere?

a. ALMA

b. SALT

c. the Arecibo telescope

d. the Hubble telescope

ANSWERS: 1. b; 2. c; 3. c; 4. a; 5. d; 6. b; 7. a; 8. d; 9. c; 10. c; 11. b; 12. b

FIND OUT MORE

Fascinated by space and want to explore further? Try these books and websites to shine even more light on the subject.

OUTSTANDING WEBSITES

Kids: Ask your parents for permission to search online.

http://www.nasa.gov/
The superstar of space sites! Tour the universe and discover the latest research and missions.

http://www.space.com/
Get the latest news on everything space-related.

http://hubblesite.org/
See what Hubble sees, and learn what it means to astronomers.

FAR-OUT PLACES TO VISIT

Kennedy Space Center Visitor Complex
Cape Canaveral, Florida, U.S.A.

Space Center Houston
Houston, Texas, U.S.A.

W. M. Keck Observatory
Mauna Kea, Hawai'i, U.S.A.

McDonald Park Dark Sky Park
Abbotsford, British Columbia, Canada

FUN FLICKS

Get your space fix with these classic space-related films.
Kids: Ask your parents for permission to watch.

Cosmos: A Spacetime Odyssey National Geographic, 2014

Hubble's Amazing Universe National Geographic, 2008

Monster Black Holes National Geographic, 2008

Known Universe National Geographic, 2011

Star Wars: Episode V: The Empire Strikes Back

The Right Stuff

Apollo 13

OUT-OF-THIS-WORLD BOOKS

Space Encyclopedia: A Tour of Our Solar System and Beyond
by David A. Aguilar
National Geographic Kids, 2013

National Geographic Little Kids First Big Book of Space
by Catherine D. Hughes
National Geographic Kids, 2012

13 Planets: The Latest View of the Solar System
by David A. Aguilar
National Geographic Kids, 2011

BOLDFACE INDICATES ILLUSTRATIONS.

Acknowledgment: Special thanks to Michael Szasz for researching and co-authoring this work.

NG Staff for This Book
Shelby Alinsky, *Project Editor*
James Hiscott, Jr., *Art Director*
Lori Epstein, *Senior Photo Editor*
Carl Mehler, *Director of Maps*
Paige Towler, *Editorial Assistant*
Sanjida Rashid and Rachel Kenny, *Design Production Assistants*
Colm McKeveny, *Rights Clearance Specialist*
Grace Hill, *Managing Editor*
Mike O'Connor, *Production Editor*
Lewis R. Bassford, *Production Manager*
Rachel Faulise, *Manager, Production Services*
Susan Borke, *Legal and Business Affairs*

Published by the National Geographic Society
Gary E. Knell, *President and CEO*
John M. Fahey, *Chairman of the Board*
Melina Gerosa Bellows, *Chief Education Officer*
Declan Moore, *Chief Media Officer*
Hector Sierra, *Senior Vice President and General Manager, Book Division*

Senior Management Team, Kids Publishing and Media
Nancy Laties Feresten, *Senior Vice President*
Jennifer Emmett, *Vice President, Editorial Director, Kids Books*
Julie Vosburgh Agnone, *Vice President, Editorial Operations*
Rachel Buchholz, *Editor and Vice President,* NG Kids *magazine*
Michelle Sullivan, *Vice President, Kids Digital*
Eva Absher-Schantz, *Design Director*
Jay Sumner, *Photo Director*
Hannah August, *Marketing Director*
R. Gary Colbert, *Production Director*

Digital
Anne McCormack, *Director*
Laura Goertzel, Sara Zeglin, *Producers*
Emma Rigney, *Creative Producer*
Bianca Bowman, *Assistant Producer*
Natalie Jones, *Senior Product Manager*

Editorial, Design, and Production by Plan B Book Packagers

Captions
Cover: Light echoes from a supergiant star in this telescope image.
Page 1: Clouds of gas surround stars deep in the universe.
Pages 2–3: An astronaut does maintenance outside the ISS.

The National Geographic Society is one of the world's largest nonprofit scientific and educational organizations. Founded in 1888 to "increase and diffuse geographic knowledge," the Society's mission is to inspire people to care about the planet. It reaches more than 400 million people worldwide each month through its official journal, *National Geographic,* and other magazines; National Geographic Channel; television documentaries; music; radio; films; books; DVDs; maps; exhibitions; live events; school publishing programs; interactive media; and merchandise. National Geographic has funded more than 10,000 scientific research, conservation, and exploration projects and supports an education program promoting geographic literacy.

For more information, please visit nationalgeographic.com, call 1-800-NGS LINE (647-5463), or write to the following address:
National Geographic Society
1145 17th Street N.W.
Washington, D.C. 20036-4688 U.S.A.

Visit us online at nationalgeographic.com/books

For librarians and teachers: ngchildrensbooks.org

More for kids from National Geographic:
kids.nationalgeographic.com

For information about special discounts for bulk purchases, please contact National Geographic Books Special Sales: ngspecsales@ngs.org

For rights or permissions inquiries, please contact National Geographic Books Subsidiary Rights: ngbookrights@ngs.org

Paperback ISBN: 978-1-4263-2074-3
Reinforced library binding ISBN: 978-1-4263-2075-0

Printed in Hong Kong
15/THK/1